# Postage Book

| Date | Name and Address | Brief Description | Cost |
|------|------------------|-------------------|------|
|      |                  |                   |      |
|      |                  |                   |      |
|      |                  |                   |      |
|      |                  |                   |      |
|      |                  |                   |      |
|      |                  |                   |      |
|      |                  |                   |      |
|      |                  |                   |      |
|      |                  |                   |      |
|      |                  |                   |      |
|      |                  |                   |      |
|      |                  |                   |      |

| Date | Name and Address | Brief Description | Cost |
|------|------------------|-------------------|------|
|      |                  |                   |      |
|      |                  |                   |      |
|      |                  |                   |      |
|      |                  |                   |      |
|      |                  |                   |      |
|      |                  |                   |      |
|      |                  |                   |      |
|      |                  |                   |      |
|      |                  |                   |      |
|      |                  |                   |      |
|      |                  |                   |      |
|      |                  |                   |      |

| Date | Name and Address | Brief Description | Cost |
|------|------------------|-------------------|------|
|      |                  |                   |      |
|      |                  |                   |      |
|      |                  |                   |      |
|      |                  |                   |      |
|      |                  |                   |      |
|      |                  |                   |      |
|      |                  |                   |      |
|      |                  |                   |      |
|      |                  |                   |      |
|      |                  |                   |      |
|      |                  |                   |      |
|      |                  |                   |      |

| Date | Name and Address | Brief Description | Cost |
|------|------------------|-------------------|------|
|      |                  |                   |      |
|      |                  |                   |      |
|      |                  |                   |      |
|      |                  |                   |      |
|      |                  |                   |      |
|      |                  |                   |      |
|      |                  |                   |      |
|      |                  |                   |      |
|      |                  |                   |      |
|      |                  |                   |      |
|      |                  |                   |      |
|      |                  |                   |      |

| Date | Name and Address | Brief Description | Cost |
|------|------------------|-------------------|------|
|      |                  |                   |      |
|      |                  |                   |      |
|      |                  |                   |      |
|      |                  |                   |      |
|      |                  |                   |      |
|      |                  |                   |      |
|      |                  |                   |      |
|      |                  |                   |      |
|      |                  |                   |      |
|      |                  |                   |      |
|      |                  |                   |      |
|      |                  |                   |      |

| Date | Name and Address | Brief Description | Cost |
|---|---|---|---|
|  |  |  |  |
|  |  |  |  |
|  |  |  |  |
|  |  |  |  |
|  |  |  |  |
|  |  |  |  |
|  |  |  |  |
|  |  |  |  |
|  |  |  |  |
|  |  |  |  |
|  |  |  |  |
|  |  |  |  |

| Date | Name and Address | Brief Description | Cost |
|------|------------------|-------------------|------|
|      |                  |                   |      |
|      |                  |                   |      |
|      |                  |                   |      |
|      |                  |                   |      |
|      |                  |                   |      |
|      |                  |                   |      |
|      |                  |                   |      |
|      |                  |                   |      |
|      |                  |                   |      |
|      |                  |                   |      |
|      |                  |                   |      |

| Date | Name and Address | Brief Description | Cost |
|------|------------------|-------------------|------|
|      |                  |                   |      |
|      |                  |                   |      |
|      |                  |                   |      |
|      |                  |                   |      |
|      |                  |                   |      |
|      |                  |                   |      |
|      |                  |                   |      |
|      |                  |                   |      |
|      |                  |                   |      |
|      |                  |                   |      |
|      |                  |                   |      |
|      |                  |                   |      |

| Date | Name and Address | Brief Description | Cost |
|------|------------------|-------------------|------|
|      |                  |                   |      |
|      |                  |                   |      |
|      |                  |                   |      |
|      |                  |                   |      |
|      |                  |                   |      |
|      |                  |                   |      |
|      |                  |                   |      |
|      |                  |                   |      |
|      |                  |                   |      |
|      |                  |                   |      |
|      |                  |                   |      |
|      |                  |                   |      |

| Date | Name and Address | Brief Description | Cost |
|---|---|---|---|
|  |  |  |  |
|  |  |  |  |
|  |  |  |  |
|  |  |  |  |
|  |  |  |  |
|  |  |  |  |
|  |  |  |  |
|  |  |  |  |
|  |  |  |  |
|  |  |  |  |
|  |  |  |  |
|  |  |  |  |

| Date | Name and Address | Brief Description | Cost |
|------|------------------|-------------------|------|
|      |                  |                   |      |
|      |                  |                   |      |
|      |                  |                   |      |
|      |                  |                   |      |
|      |                  |                   |      |
|      |                  |                   |      |
|      |                  |                   |      |
|      |                  |                   |      |
|      |                  |                   |      |
|      |                  |                   |      |
|      |                  |                   |      |
|      |                  |                   |      |

| Date | Name and Address | Brief Description | Cost |
|---|---|---|---|
| | | | |
| | | | |
| | | | |
| | | | |
| | | | |
| | | | |
| | | | |
| | | | |
| | | | |
| | | | |
| | | | |
| | | | |

| Date | Name and Address | Brief Description | Cost |
|------|------------------|-------------------|------|
|      |                  |                   |      |
|      |                  |                   |      |
|      |                  |                   |      |
|      |                  |                   |      |
|      |                  |                   |      |
|      |                  |                   |      |
|      |                  |                   |      |
|      |                  |                   |      |
|      |                  |                   |      |
|      |                  |                   |      |
|      |                  |                   |      |

| Date | Name and Address | Brief Description | Cost |
|------|------------------|-------------------|------|
|      |                  |                   |      |
|      |                  |                   |      |
|      |                  |                   |      |
|      |                  |                   |      |
|      |                  |                   |      |
|      |                  |                   |      |
|      |                  |                   |      |
|      |                  |                   |      |
|      |                  |                   |      |
|      |                  |                   |      |
|      |                  |                   |      |
|      |                  |                   |      |

| Date | Name and Address | Brief Description | Cost |
|------|------------------|-------------------|------|
|      |                  |                   |      |
|      |                  |                   |      |
|      |                  |                   |      |
|      |                  |                   |      |
|      |                  |                   |      |
|      |                  |                   |      |
|      |                  |                   |      |
|      |                  |                   |      |
|      |                  |                   |      |
|      |                  |                   |      |
|      |                  |                   |      |
|      |                  |                   |      |

| Date | Name and Address | Brief Description | Cost |
|------|------------------|-------------------|------|
|      |                  |                   |      |
|      |                  |                   |      |
|      |                  |                   |      |
|      |                  |                   |      |
|      |                  |                   |      |
|      |                  |                   |      |
|      |                  |                   |      |
|      |                  |                   |      |
|      |                  |                   |      |
|      |                  |                   |      |
|      |                  |                   |      |
|      |                  |                   |      |

| Date | Name and Address | Brief Description | Cost |
|---|---|---|---|
| | | | |
| | | | |
| | | | |
| | | | |
| | | | |
| | | | |
| | | | |
| | | | |
| | | | |
| | | | |
| | | | |
| | | | |

| Date | Name and Address | Brief Description | Cost |
|------|------------------|-------------------|------|
|      |                  |                   |      |
|      |                  |                   |      |
|      |                  |                   |      |
|      |                  |                   |      |
|      |                  |                   |      |
|      |                  |                   |      |
|      |                  |                   |      |
|      |                  |                   |      |
|      |                  |                   |      |
|      |                  |                   |      |
|      |                  |                   |      |
|      |                  |                   |      |

| Date | Name and Address | Brief Description | Cost |
|---|---|---|---|
| | | | |
| | | | |
| | | | |
| | | | |
| | | | |
| | | | |
| | | | |
| | | | |
| | | | |
| | | | |
| | | | |
| | | | |

| Date | Name and Address | Brief Description | Cost |
|---|---|---|---|
|  |  |  |  |
|  |  |  |  |
|  |  |  |  |
|  |  |  |  |
|  |  |  |  |
|  |  |  |  |
|  |  |  |  |
|  |  |  |  |
|  |  |  |  |
|  |  |  |  |
|  |  |  |  |

| Date | Name and Address | Brief Description | Cost |
|------|------------------|-------------------|------|
|      |                  |                   |      |
|      |                  |                   |      |
|      |                  |                   |      |
|      |                  |                   |      |
|      |                  |                   |      |
|      |                  |                   |      |
|      |                  |                   |      |
|      |                  |                   |      |
|      |                  |                   |      |
|      |                  |                   |      |
|      |                  |                   |      |
|      |                  |                   |      |

| Date | Name and Address | Brief Description | Cost |
|------|------------------|-------------------|------|
|      |                  |                   |      |
|      |                  |                   |      |
|      |                  |                   |      |
|      |                  |                   |      |
|      |                  |                   |      |
|      |                  |                   |      |
|      |                  |                   |      |
|      |                  |                   |      |
|      |                  |                   |      |
|      |                  |                   |      |
|      |                  |                   |      |

| Date | Name and Address | Brief Description | Cost |
|---|---|---|---|
| | | | |
| | | | |
| | | | |
| | | | |
| | | | |
| | | | |
| | | | |
| | | | |
| | | | |
| | | | |
| | | | |
| | | | |

| Date | Name and Address | Brief Description | Cost |
|---|---|---|---|
|  |  |  |  |
|  |  |  |  |
|  |  |  |  |
|  |  |  |  |
|  |  |  |  |
|  |  |  |  |
|  |  |  |  |
|  |  |  |  |
|  |  |  |  |
|  |  |  |  |
|  |  |  |  |
|  |  |  |  |

| Date | Name and Address | Brief Description | Cost |
|---|---|---|---|
|  |  |  |  |
|  |  |  |  |
|  |  |  |  |
|  |  |  |  |
|  |  |  |  |
|  |  |  |  |
|  |  |  |  |
|  |  |  |  |
|  |  |  |  |
|  |  |  |  |
|  |  |  |  |
|  |  |  |  |

| Date | Name and Address | Brief Description | Cost |
|---|---|---|---|
| | | | |
| | | | |
| | | | |
| | | | |
| | | | |
| | | | |
| | | | |
| | | | |
| | | | |
| | | | |
| | | | |
| | | | |

| Date | Name and Address | Brief Description | Cost |
|---|---|---|---|
| | | | |
| | | | |
| | | | |
| | | | |
| | | | |
| | | | |
| | | | |
| | | | |
| | | | |
| | | | |
| | | | |
| | | | |

| Date | Name and Address | Brief Description | Cost |
|------|------------------|-------------------|------|
|      |                  |                   |      |
|      |                  |                   |      |
|      |                  |                   |      |
|      |                  |                   |      |
|      |                  |                   |      |
|      |                  |                   |      |
|      |                  |                   |      |
|      |                  |                   |      |
|      |                  |                   |      |
|      |                  |                   |      |
|      |                  |                   |      |
|      |                  |                   |      |

| Date | Name and Address | Brief Description | Cost |
|------|------------------|-------------------|------|
|      |                  |                   |      |
|      |                  |                   |      |
|      |                  |                   |      |
|      |                  |                   |      |
|      |                  |                   |      |
|      |                  |                   |      |
|      |                  |                   |      |
|      |                  |                   |      |
|      |                  |                   |      |
|      |                  |                   |      |
|      |                  |                   |      |
|      |                  |                   |      |

| Date | Name and Address | Brief Description | Cost |
|---|---|---|---|
| | | | |
| | | | |
| | | | |
| | | | |
| | | | |
| | | | |
| | | | |
| | | | |
| | | | |
| | | | |
| | | | |
| | | | |

| Date | Name and Address | Brief Description | Cost |
|------|------------------|-------------------|------|
|      |                  |                   |      |
|      |                  |                   |      |
|      |                  |                   |      |
|      |                  |                   |      |
|      |                  |                   |      |
|      |                  |                   |      |
|      |                  |                   |      |
|      |                  |                   |      |
|      |                  |                   |      |
|      |                  |                   |      |
|      |                  |                   |      |
|      |                  |                   |      |

| Date | Name and Address | Brief Description | Cost |
|---|---|---|---|
|  |  |  |  |
|  |  |  |  |
|  |  |  |  |
|  |  |  |  |
|  |  |  |  |
|  |  |  |  |
|  |  |  |  |
|  |  |  |  |
|  |  |  |  |
|  |  |  |  |
|  |  |  |  |
|  |  |  |  |

| Date | Name and Address | Brief Description | Cost |
|------|------------------|-------------------|------|
|      |                  |                   |      |
|      |                  |                   |      |
|      |                  |                   |      |
|      |                  |                   |      |
|      |                  |                   |      |
|      |                  |                   |      |
|      |                  |                   |      |
|      |                  |                   |      |
|      |                  |                   |      |
|      |                  |                   |      |
|      |                  |                   |      |

| Date | Name and Address | Brief Description | Cost |
|------|------------------|-------------------|------|
|      |                  |                   |      |
|      |                  |                   |      |
|      |                  |                   |      |
|      |                  |                   |      |
|      |                  |                   |      |
|      |                  |                   |      |
|      |                  |                   |      |
|      |                  |                   |      |
|      |                  |                   |      |
|      |                  |                   |      |
|      |                  |                   |      |
|      |                  |                   |      |

| Date | Name and Address | Brief Description | Cost |
|---|---|---|---|
| | | | |
| | | | |
| | | | |
| | | | |
| | | | |
| | | | |
| | | | |
| | | | |
| | | | |
| | | | |
| | | | |
| | | | |

| Date | Name and Address | Brief Description | Cost |
|---|---|---|---|
|  |  |  |  |
|  |  |  |  |
|  |  |  |  |
|  |  |  |  |
|  |  |  |  |
|  |  |  |  |
|  |  |  |  |
|  |  |  |  |
|  |  |  |  |
|  |  |  |  |
|  |  |  |  |

| Date | Name and Address | Brief Description | Cost |
|---|---|---|---|
|  |  |  |  |
|  |  |  |  |
|  |  |  |  |
|  |  |  |  |
|  |  |  |  |
|  |  |  |  |
|  |  |  |  |
|  |  |  |  |
|  |  |  |  |
|  |  |  |  |
|  |  |  |  |
|  |  |  |  |

| Date | Name and Address | Brief Description | Cost |
|---|---|---|---|
|  |  |  |  |
|  |  |  |  |
|  |  |  |  |
|  |  |  |  |
|  |  |  |  |
|  |  |  |  |
|  |  |  |  |
|  |  |  |  |
|  |  |  |  |
|  |  |  |  |
|  |  |  |  |
|  |  |  |  |

| Date | Name and Address | Brief Description | Cost |
|---|---|---|---|
| | | | |
| | | | |
| | | | |
| | | | |
| | | | |
| | | | |
| | | | |
| | | | |
| | | | |
| | | | |
| | | | |
| | | | |

| Date | Name and Address | Brief Description | Cost |
|------|------------------|-------------------|------|
|      |                  |                   |      |
|      |                  |                   |      |
|      |                  |                   |      |
|      |                  |                   |      |
|      |                  |                   |      |
|      |                  |                   |      |
|      |                  |                   |      |
|      |                  |                   |      |
|      |                  |                   |      |
|      |                  |                   |      |
|      |                  |                   |      |
|      |                  |                   |      |

| Date | Name and Address | Brief Description | Cost |
|---|---|---|---|
| | | | |
| | | | |
| | | | |
| | | | |
| | | | |
| | | | |
| | | | |
| | | | |
| | | | |
| | | | |
| | | | |
| | | | |

| Date | Name and Address | Brief Description | Cost |
|------|------------------|-------------------|------|
|      |                  |                   |      |
|      |                  |                   |      |
|      |                  |                   |      |
|      |                  |                   |      |
|      |                  |                   |      |
|      |                  |                   |      |
|      |                  |                   |      |
|      |                  |                   |      |
|      |                  |                   |      |
|      |                  |                   |      |
|      |                  |                   |      |
|      |                  |                   |      |

| Date | Name and Address | Brief Description | Cost |
|------|------------------|-------------------|------|
|      |                  |                   |      |
|      |                  |                   |      |
|      |                  |                   |      |
|      |                  |                   |      |
|      |                  |                   |      |
|      |                  |                   |      |
|      |                  |                   |      |
|      |                  |                   |      |
|      |                  |                   |      |
|      |                  |                   |      |
|      |                  |                   |      |
|      |                  |                   |      |

| Date | Name and Address | Brief Description | Cost |
|------|------------------|-------------------|------|
|      |                  |                   |      |
|      |                  |                   |      |
|      |                  |                   |      |
|      |                  |                   |      |
|      |                  |                   |      |
|      |                  |                   |      |
|      |                  |                   |      |
|      |                  |                   |      |
|      |                  |                   |      |
|      |                  |                   |      |
|      |                  |                   |      |
|      |                  |                   |      |

| Date | Name and Address | Brief Description | Cost |
|------|------------------|-------------------|------|
|      |                  |                   |      |
|      |                  |                   |      |
|      |                  |                   |      |
|      |                  |                   |      |
|      |                  |                   |      |
|      |                  |                   |      |
|      |                  |                   |      |
|      |                  |                   |      |
|      |                  |                   |      |
|      |                  |                   |      |
|      |                  |                   |      |
|      |                  |                   |      |

| Date | Name and Address | Brief Description | Cost |
|------|------------------|-------------------|------|
|      |                  |                   |      |
|      |                  |                   |      |
|      |                  |                   |      |
|      |                  |                   |      |
|      |                  |                   |      |
|      |                  |                   |      |
|      |                  |                   |      |
|      |                  |                   |      |
|      |                  |                   |      |
|      |                  |                   |      |
|      |                  |                   |      |
|      |                  |                   |      |

| Date | Name and Address | Brief Description | Cost |
|------|------------------|-------------------|------|
|      |                  |                   |      |
|      |                  |                   |      |
|      |                  |                   |      |
|      |                  |                   |      |
|      |                  |                   |      |
|      |                  |                   |      |
|      |                  |                   |      |
|      |                  |                   |      |
|      |                  |                   |      |
|      |                  |                   |      |
|      |                  |                   |      |
|      |                  |                   |      |

| Date | Name and Address | Brief Description | Cost |
|---|---|---|---|
| | | | |
| | | | |
| | | | |
| | | | |
| | | | |
| | | | |
| | | | |
| | | | |
| | | | |
| | | | |
| | | | |

| Date | Name and Address | Brief Description | Cost |
|---|---|---|---|
| | | | |
| | | | |
| | | | |
| | | | |
| | | | |
| | | | |
| | | | |
| | | | |
| | | | |
| | | | |
| | | | |
| | | | |

| Date | Name and Address | Brief Description | Cost |
|---|---|---|---|
|  |  |  |  |
|  |  |  |  |
|  |  |  |  |
|  |  |  |  |
|  |  |  |  |
|  |  |  |  |
|  |  |  |  |
|  |  |  |  |
|  |  |  |  |
|  |  |  |  |
|  |  |  |  |
|  |  |  |  |

www.ingramcontent.com/pod-product-compliance
Lightning Source LLC
Chambersburg PA
CBHW062202220526
45470CB00009B/2901